Big and Bigger

by
David Orme

Thunderbolts

Big and Bigger
by David Orme

Illustrated by Martin Roy

Published by Ransom Publishing Ltd.
Radley House, 8 St. Cross Road, Winchester, Hants. SO23 9HX, UK
www.ransom.co.uk

ISBN   978 178127 059 2
First published in 2013

Copyright © 2013 Ransom Publishing Ltd.

Illustrations copyright © 2013 Martin Roy
'Get the Facts' section - images copyright: cover, prelims, passim – Wvermaat, txd, NASA, Caelio; pp 6/7 - Ricardo Liberato, Nicolas Lannuzel, Cubbie_n_Vegas, Maurice King; pp 8/9 - A. Kniesel, Wvermaat; pp 10/11 - Paul Joseph, Aneb, Tommounsey; pp 12/13 - dawvon, Nggsc, adisa; pp 14/15 - Matej Hudovernik, Liz, Neal Parish; pp 16/17 - Quentin Douchet, Florian Lindner; pp 18/19 - Stephen & Katherine; pp 20/21 - Kati Neudert, Simone van den Berg, Justin Sneddon, Angelika Schwarz, technotr; pp 22/23 - Hbcreuz, Amsterdamman, Sami99tr; p 36 - Citizen59.

A CIP catalogue record of this book is available from the British Library.

All rights reserved. No part of this publication may be reproduced, stored in a retrieval system, or transmitted, in any form or by any means, electronic, mechanical, photocopying, recording or otherwise, without the prior permission of the publishers.

The rights of David Orme to be identified as the author and of Martin Roy to be identified as the illustrator of this Work have been asserted by them in accordance with sections 77 and 78 of the Copyright, Design and Patents Act 1988.

page 5

page 25

Big and Bigger: The Facts